INTERNET

Published by Smart Apple Media
123 South Broad Street
Mankato, Minnesota 56001

Photos: pages 8-9–CORBIS; page 10–CORBIS/Hulton-
Deutsch Collection; page 11–CORBIS/Roger Ressmeyer;
page 23–Portions © Netscape Communications Corp.,
1998. All Rights Reserved. Netscape, Netscape Naviga-
tor and the Netscape N logo, are registered trademarks
of Netscape in the United States and other countries;
page 30–CORBIS/Bettmann

Design and Production: EvansDay Design

Library of Congress Cataloging-in-Publication Data
Vander Hook, Sue, 1949–
Internet / by Sue Vander Hook
p. cm. – (Making contact)
Includes index.
Summary: Examines the origin, uses, rules and guide-
lines, and possible future of the Internet as a tool for
communication and the sharing of information.
ISBN 1-887068-61-9
1. Internet (Computer network)—Juvenile literature.
[1. Internet (Computer network)] I. Title. II. Series:
Making contact (Mankato, Minn.)

TK5105.875.I57V36   1999
004.67'8—dc21   98-20886

First edition

9 8 7 6 5 4 3 2 1

INTERNET

MAKING

CONTACT

SUE VANDER HOOK

EVERYWHERE WE TURN, WE HEAR about the Internet. It is a complex system that is underground, in telephone lines, and in millions of computers and glass tubes. It is a massive web that reaches to all corners of the earth; schools, businesses, governments, universities, and homes have all become a part of the "Net." The Internet has been called the information superhighway, because it lets people travel through the world of information at incredible speeds. No person, company, or government runs the Internet, and no one owns it. Its uses are now as numerous as its users. And although the 1990s have seen it grow at an explosive rate, today's Internet promises to be just the beginning of this new universe of information.

Today, people throughout the world communicate by computer. They can send information thousands of miles in an instant, bring encyclopedia entries to their home computer screens, or view colorful photographs at the touch of a key. Computer users can play music and watch videos with the click of a **mouse**. People can even hear and see each other live on their computers. The connection shared by all these people is called the Internet.

To understand the structure of the Internet, picture a spider web. The spider spins its silk one strand at a time, attaching each strand to the next one to make a wide web. The Internet is a huge web of computers, cables, and people. Millions of telephone cables form the web-like structure that reaches around the entire world. Messages and information travel at incredible speeds through tiny glass tubes inside these cables.

The road to this information superhighway was paved by several key inventions over the last two centuries. Worldwide communication actually began in 1838 when Samuel Morse invented the telegraph, the first method of sending messages electronically. When a

Samuel Morse invented the telegraph in 1838. But it was British inventors William Cooke and Charles Wheatstone who came up with the idea. In 1837, they sent an electric current down five wires to needles that pointed to letters and numbers on a panel. Morse's telegraph needed only one wire.

7

✳ FIBER-OPTIC WIRES HELP FORM A WEB OF INFORMATION THAT ENCIRCLES THE EARTH.

telegraph operator pressed a key, an electric impulse was sent over wires to another telegraph. Short and long taps of the key, called dots and dashes, made up the code for each letter of the alphabet. Operators used the code—called Morse code—to send messages to any destination connected by telegraph wires. In 1858, workers finished laying the first cable across the floor of the Atlantic Ocean. This transatlantic cable connected North America and Europe by electric wires for the first time, allowing people on both continents to communicate using the telegraph.

8

* SAMUEL MORSE, THE FOUNDING FATHER OF LONG-DISTANCE ELECTRONIC COMMUNICATION.

In 1867, American newspaperman and inventor Christopher Sholes invented the modern typewriter. Though quite primitive by today's standards, the invention gave millions of people the opportunity to learn to type, a skill that was transferable to later computer keyboards.

When Alexander Graham Bell introduced the telephone in 1876, his invention opened up a whole new way of communicating. The telephone sent human voices over electric wires. As telephone wires were installed around the world, more people could talk to each other from greater distances.

Sound was first recorded in 1889 when Thomas Edison invented the phonograph.

9

✳ THE CABLE LAID ACROSS THE ATLANTIC OCEAN IN 1858 CONNECTED DISTANT CONTINENTS FOR THE FIRST TIME.

George Eastman, the founder of Kodak cameras, created photographic film that same year. When people began using sound and photography together, the stage was set for motion pictures, television, and videos.

In 1894, Guglielmo Marconi developed the radio, and wireless communication was born. Radio sent invisible signals through the air from one antenna to another, bringing news, music, and entertaining programs into many homes. Little did these inventors know that their discoveries were laying a foundation for the Internet.

✳ GUGLIELMO MARCONI, THE MAN RESPONSIBLE FOR THE BIRTH OF RADIO COMMUNICATION.

AGENCY
NETWORK
MANAGEMENT
CENTER

NETWORK

to connect computers using wires,
cables, or telephone lines

COMPUTER NETWORK

computers connected by wires,
cables, or telephone lines

The first computer in North America was built in 1939. Less than 30 years later, computers were **networked**, or connected together by wires and cables. The United States military was the first to develop a **computer network**. The military wanted to make sure that important information would not be lost in the event of a nuclear war. In the late 1960s, the u.s. Department of Defense designed the Advanced Research Projects Agency Network, or ARPAnet. This network started as a way of connecting military computers, allowing them to share information and send messages to each other. In a war, communication between computers would be hard to interrupt; even if several computers were destroyed, a computer in another location would retain the important information.

II

* COMPUTER NETWORKS, INITIALLY DEVELOPED BY THE U.S. MILITARY, ARE A CRITICAL PART OF MANY MODERN BUSINESSES.

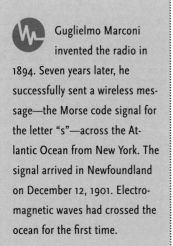
Government agencies then began helping universities network their computers. Technology improved at a fast pace. By 1972, people were using **e-mail**, or electronic mail, to send messages and information back and forth. Newspaper and magazine writers began to write about information highways, predicting that "global virtual communities" would emerge in the future.

That future became a reality sooner than anyone expected. People wanted to connect with computers farther away, so telephone lines became part of computer networks. Businesses, schools, and libraries began connecting. **Host computers** soon offered connections to individual users. A host computer is like the host of a party. A party host takes care of guests who come to visit, serving them and making them feel welcome. Likewise, a host computer takes care of people who visit by computer, serving them by letting them use the host's connection and address.

As individuals started using host computers, the web of connections extended to more and more of the world. The creators of ARPAnet stepped aside, allowing the worldwide network of the Internet to take over. What began as a way to protect information had instead become a worldwide effort to make information available.

13

✳ E-MAIL HAS BECOME THE FASTEST AND MOST CONVENIENT MEANS OF WRITTEN COMMUNICATION TODAY.

The Rules of the Internet

Computer scientists who designed the Internet quickly ran into a problem: there were many different kinds of computers. If computers were to be connected worldwide, someone had to devise a way for all kinds of computers to understand each other.

At first, there was chaos. Each computer network was using its own "language," or codes, so one group of computers could not communicate with other groups. ARPAnet solved this problem in 1973 by developing a standard computer language called **Internet protocols**. A protocol is a rule that determines how something is done. The rules of a game tell how many people can play, what players can and cannot do, and how to keep score and win. Once players know the rules, they can play with people they don't even know. Internet protocols serve the same purpose.

The first Internet protocol is called just that—Internet Protocol, or IP. This rule states that every computer connected to the Internet must have an address containing four sets of numbers separated by periods, such as 109.111.63.432. To make it easier to remember, each

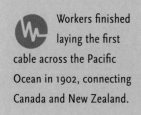

Workers finished laying the first cable across the Pacific Ocean in 1902, connecting Canada and New Zealand.

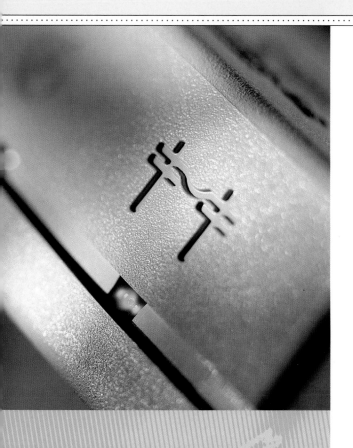

address has an alphabetical name as well, such as *host.computer.com.*

The other basic protocol is called Transmission Control Protocol, or TCP. This rule states that information sent by computer users is broken into small chunks. Each chunk is numbered in sequence. A computer device called a **modem** gets the information ready to send. When another computer receives these chunks of information, its modem puts them back in order.

Every computer user on the Internet also has a personal address that is used

INTERNET PROTOCOLS

universal rules that determine how the Internet works

MODEM

a device that can change computer information to digital code and vice versa; it allows computer users to communicate with each other using phone lines

✳ WITH A MODEM, COMPUTER USERS CAN SEND INFORMATION OR RECEIVE IT FROM ALL PARTS OF THE WORLD.

to connect to the Internet or to send e-mail. The address begins with a **user ID** or user name. For example, someone whose last name is Anderson may choose ander as a user name. This is followed by an *at* symbol that looks like this: @. Next comes the address of the host computer, which could look like this: host.computer.com. The last part of the host address indicates whether the host computer belongs to a business, government, or an organization such as a school. The host address we've shown ends with .com, indicating that it belongs to a commercial business. The personal address ander@host.computer.com provides all the information needed for a user to connect to the Internet.

The word "laser" is an acronym, a word formed from the first letters of several other words. The letters in "laser" stand for **L**ight **A**mplification by **S**timulated **E**mission of **R**adiation.

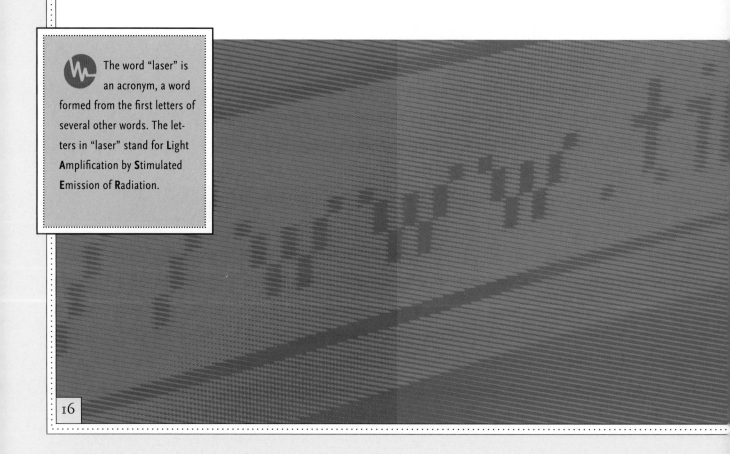

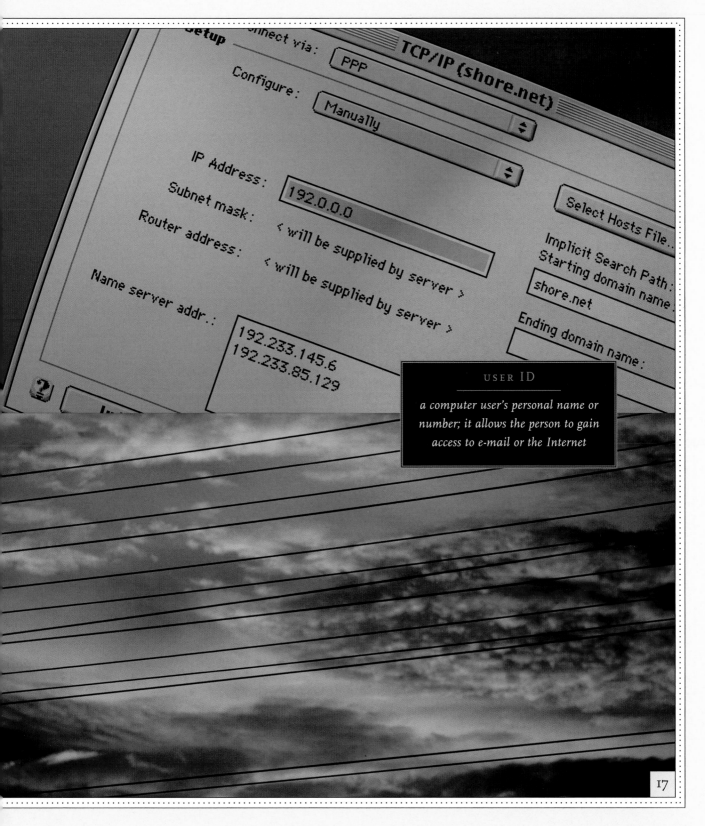

TCP/IP (shore.net)

Connect via: PPP

Configure: Manually

IP Address: 192.0.0.0
Subnet mask: < will be supplied by server >
Router address: < will be supplied by server >
Name server addr.:
192.233.145.6
192.233.85.129

Select Hosts File...

Implicit Search Path:
Starting domain name:
shore.net

Ending domain name:

17

✳ ONCE USED ONLY TO TRANSMIT VERBAL COMMUNICATION, TELEPHONE LINES NOW CONNECT INTERNET USERS AS WELL.

Traveling Through Cyberspace

After a computer has been connected to a host, the computer user can enter the world of **cyberspace**. This electronic world is everywhere your computer takes you on the Internet; it includes your colorful computer screen and the millions of telephone lines and modems sending and receiving **data**, or

information. Cyberspace is where billions of **bits** of information are exchanged.

Since actual words, pictures, and sounds cannot be sent through wires and cables, computers use a number-based code called **digital language**. Computer language is also a **binary code**, which means that it is based on two numbers. Computers combine the numbers 1 and 0. Each number is called a bit; eight bits make up a **byte**. Every letter of the alphabet is coded in bits. For example, in the binary digital code, the letter "a" is 00001, "b" is 00010, and so on.

This code is sent to other computers by laser signals carried by cables. It is like a secret message a person might send by flashlight. Turning the flashlight on and off in a certain pattern creates the message, and the person receiving the message must know the secret code to understand the pattern of flashes. In the same way, a

Because computers are connected all over the world, users need a security system to prevent people from accessing information from another user's computer. In this security system, each user has a secret password. No one but the computer's owner or user should know the password.

CYBERSPACE
*everywhere a computer takes
users on the Internet*

DATA
*information; it can be sent across
the Internet
through computers*

BIT
*the smallest piece of information
a computer can understand*

DIGITAL LANGUAGE
*computer language based
on numbers*

✳ MODERN CABLES CAN CARRY MILLIONS OF LASER SIGNALS ACROSS THE WORLD WITHIN SECONDS.

computer sends out two kinds of light signals: on, represented by the number 1, or off, represented by 0.

If a computer user sends the letter "t" to another computer, the user's modem would first change it to these binary digits: 11011. The letter would then travel through cyberspace as laser signals. Since the code for "t" is 11011, the light would pulse on, on, off, on, on. When the light signals arrived at their destination, perhaps on the other side of the world, another modem would translate them back to "t."

Pictures are sent through cyberspace in a similar way. A picture is divided into millions of little pieces, or bytes. Each byte has its own binary digital code, which is sent by laser signals. When these millions of codes arrive at the picture's destination, they are translated by modem back into a picture.

Sending sound works almost the same way. However, sound is made up of many different levels, or waves. Instead of on-off light signals, sound is sent by adjustable lights, a process that works much like the dimmer switch on a light at home. The light can change from dim to bright, with many levels of brightness in between. By combining pictures and sound, the Internet can bring music videos and segments of movies to home computer screens.

After words, pictures, or sounds have been coded, the laser signals are sent through

> An e-mail message can travel thousands of miles in just a few seconds. Because e-mail is so fast, people have given traditional, stamped mail a new nickname: "snail-mail."

telephone cables at an incredible speed. Many of these cables contain tiny glass tubes called **optical fibers**. Although each fiber is no thicker than a human hair, it can conduct millions of bits of information per second, handling thousands of two-way communications simultaneously. Billions of high-speed laser pulses travel through these strands of glass each day. Optical fibers carry signals farther and faster than regular copper telephone wires, allowing e-mail messages and information to arrive at their destinations within seconds. Today, to meet the challenge of serving the growing number of Internet users, telephone companies are installing better equipment, including more fiber-optic cables.

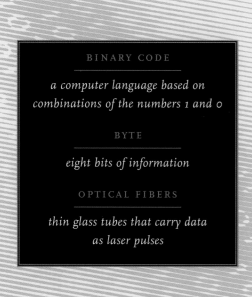

BINARY CODE
───────────
a computer language based on combinations of the numbers 1 and 0

BYTE
───────────
eight bits of information

OPTICAL FIBERS
───────────
thin glass tubes that carry data as laser pulses

21

* TINY YET POWERFUL OPTICAL FIBERS ARE QUICKLY REPLACING OLDER COMMUNICATION CABLES.

The World Wide Web

Once a person enters cyberspace, he or she has access to an almost infinite amount of information. But the first step to gathering this information is knowing where to look. There are a number of ways to go about finding things on the Internet. The most common way is through

the **World Wide Web**, often called "the Web" or "WWW" for short. It is like an on-ramp to the information superhighway.

The Web contains **search engines**, **Web sites** that use powerful programs to search for information. These sites are like travel guides—they make it easier to reach a destination in cyberspace. One click of a mouse will start the search engine looking through the entire World Wide Web for information about a specific subject. Colorful displays and interesting information quickly appear, revealing pathways to almost any subject. Sometimes users may simply start clicking on many subjects to see where they lead, jumping from one site to the next. This random exploration is often referred to as **surfing the Net**.

The idea for the Web originated in 1990. The European Particle

On January 15, 1990, one of AT&T's long-distance telephone systems crashed, leaving more than 60,000 people without telephone service for nine hours. The computerized telephone system had not crashed on its own, however. It had been made to crash by hackers, people who break into someone else's computer system illegally.

22

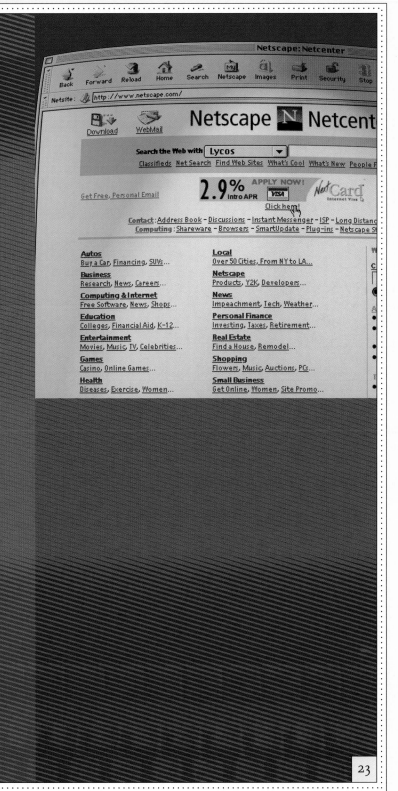

WORLD WIDE WEB

a system of accessing information on the Internet by using hypertext language and links to other Web sites

SEARCH ENGINES

Web sites that search the Internet for information on a particular subject

WEB SITE

a destination on the World Wide Web

SURFING THE NET

exploring the Internet in a random pattern by moving from one site to another

23

* MANY INTERNET PROGRAMS OFFER E-MAIL, SEARCH ENGINES, AND TOPIC DIRECTORIES ON A SINGLE WEB PAGE.

Physics Laboratory in Geneva, Switzerland, developed the Web to help researchers share documents. Scientists at the laboratory created a Web language called **hypertext**. They then wrote three new protocols so everyone could use hypertext.

The first protocol is the Universal Resource Locator, or URL, the address of the Web page. Typing a particular address takes you directly to the Web site with that address. The second protocol is Hypertext Markup Language, or HTML. This protocol controls the layout of Web pages and provides tools for information

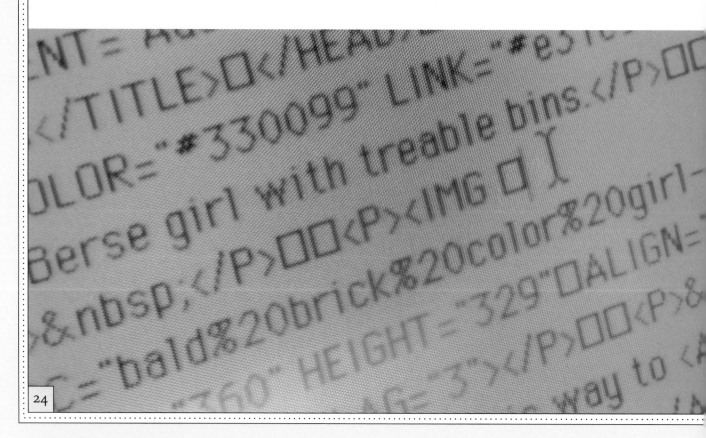

* THE WEB LANGUAGE KNOWN AS HYPERTEXT ALLOWS COMPUTER USERS EVERYWHERE TO SHARE INFORMATION.

searching. The final protocol is Hypertext Transfer Protocol, or HTTP, which controls the way that documents are requested and sent across the Internet.

These protocols are mainly used by people interested in creating Web pages. A person who wants to find information on the Web needs only to know how to type the address. The first part of a Web address is http://. This tells the computer which protocol to use in connecting with a Web site. The next part of the address is the URL, or the location of the particular Web site. For example, the address for NASA is www.nasa.gov. This address indicates that the space agency's Web site is found on the World Wide Web (www). It also tells Internet users that NASA's Web site name is

HYPERTEXT

computer language used for the World Wide Web that allows users to move quickly from one page to another

✳ EXPLORATION OF THE WEB USUALLY BEGINS WITH A SINGLE SITE ADDRESS THAT MAY BRANCH OUT IN DIFFERENT DIRECTIONS.

nasa. The last part of the address, gov, indicates that NASA is a government organization. So http://www.nasa.gov is the complete address for NASA.

Once the user arrives at a Web site, clicking on **hypertext links** leads to even more pages on the same subject. Hypertext links are words underlined on the screen; they are usually presented in a different color than the surrounding text, but a link may also be presented as a picture. For example, clicking on links while visiting http://www.nasa.gov might take the user to pictures of Mars or call up information about the space station *Mir*. It might even lead to the audio, or sound, of an astronaut talking or a video of a launch. Clicking on hypertext links is the easiest way to surf the Net.

HYPERTEXT LINKS

underlined or colored words on a Web page that connect to other pages on a related subject

ONLINE

a term that means a computer is connected to the Internet

26

In 1993, there were only 26,000 Web sites. In 1994, Pizza Hut became the first company to let people order products through a Web site. That same year, First Virtual became the world's first cyberbank, offering banking services **online**. Since then, a population explosion has hit the Web, with sites now numbering in the millions. Countless businesses and organizations do business on the Web. News agencies, magazines, weather channels, sports networks, universities, government agencies, and individuals have their own Web sites. A 1998 study indicated that more than one-third of Americans over the age of 16 were using the Internet. Information is exchanged globally on the Web every second of every day.

27

* WEB SITES DEVOTED TO SPORTS NEWS HAVE BECOME POPULAR DESTINATIONS ON THE NET.

Entering a New Era

More than 150 years have passed since the telegraph sent the first electronic message. Voices have been carried by telephone lines and radio waves for more than a century. By comparison, the Internet is still in its infancy. In its short history, the Internet has already dramatically changed the way we communicate, study, and do business. But the Internet of the future will not be the one we are using now. New technology will undoubtedly be developed to make communication better and faster.

Hints of the Internet's future can already be seen today. Frustrated by busy telephone lines, some Internet users have begun to use antennas to make their connection. The Internet may someday be wireless, sending information entirely by satellite.

The Internet may also combine computers and televisions into huge, information-entertainment centers. In fact, some people are already surfing the Net and cable television at the same time by adding TV tuners to their computers. Others are connecting their computers to their TVs with a linking device.

Someday, the Internet may translate information into almost any

The Federal Computer Investigations Committee, or FCIC, is an important organization in charge of investigating computer crimes on the Internet. The FCIC is made up of local and state police, federal agents, and the Secret Service.

29

* Radio antennas help make wireless communication possible.

language in the world. In fact, one company is currently translating a major U.S. newspaper into Spanish, Japanese, and French, and there are already many multi-lingual Web sites.

New technology will continue to expand the Internet, changing the way the world communicates. What began in 1838 as simple dots and dashes has become a complex system of lasers through cyberspace. Two people talking through wires has grown to millions of people communicating through computers. It appears that the Internet's biggest challenge in the future will be accommodating the billions of people who will want to use it.

In 1996, Internet experts formed the Internet Society. Thousands of experts from all over the world now help solve Internet problems and work on new ways to help it handle the millions of new Web sites.

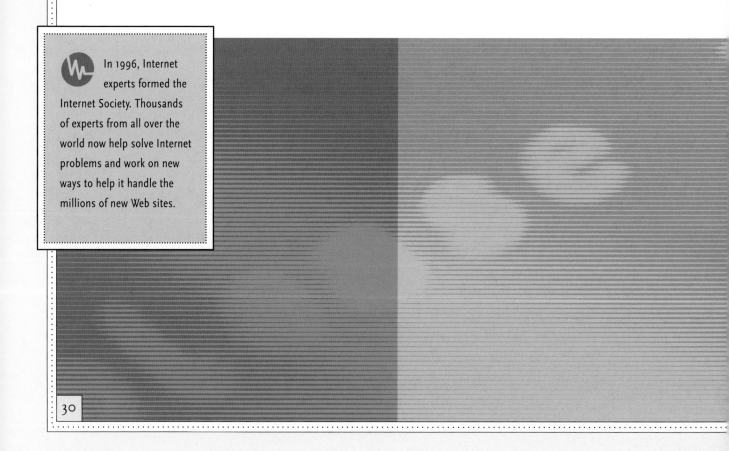

31

* The principles behind Morse's telegraph (left) have grown into a powerful means of global communication.

INDEX